Hack Craft

Clever Hacks for Everyday Life

BY

MD ABDUL MANNAN

Book Description

Unlock the art of ingenious problem-solving with **Hack Craft: Clever Hack For Everyday Solutions!**

Life's daily challenges are inevitable, but with **Hack Craft**, you'll discover how to turn small problems into creative opportunities. Packed with brilliant hacks, this guide offers practical, fun, and time-saving solutions for every corner of your life.

Inside, you'll find: • Step-by-step instructions to transform ordinary objects into extraordinary tools. • Time- and money-saving tricks for your home, travel, and beyond. • Eco-friendly ideas to live smarter and greener. • Inspiring DIY projects that unleash your inner innovator.

From fixing zippers to organizing clutter, simplifying self-care, or even surviving a camping trip, **Hack Craft** equips you with the knowledge and confidence to face life's little inconveniences with ease.

Whether you're a busy parent, a DIY enthusiast, or someone who loves clever solutions, this book is your go-to resource for mastering the art of everyday problem-solving.

Get ready to hack your way to a simpler, smarter life—one ingenious solution at a time

Table of Contents

Chapter -- Page

Chapter One

The Art of Hacking Everyday Life

Every day, we encounter small hurdles—a zipper that won't budge, a messy drawer, or a tech device acting up. These moments, while minor, disrupt our flow. But what if you could tackle each challenge with a simple, ingenious solution? Welcome to the world of life hacks—where creativity meets practicality. This book is your ultimate guide to transforming ordinary problems into extraordinary opportunities. Let's unlock the potential of everyday objects and embrace the joy of clever problem-solving.

The Everyday Struggles We All Face

Life is full of minor inconveniences that seem trivial but can feel overwhelming in the moment. A stubborn zipper, a tangled set of earphones, or a messy desk—all of these can disrupt our focus. However, these small problems often have simple solutions that can save time, reduce stress, and even spark a little joy.

Anecdote: The Stubborn Zipper

I once found myself in a rush, trying to zip up my favorite jacket before heading out the door. The zipper was stuck halfway. Frustrated, I tried pulling it harder, but it wouldn't budge. In desperation, I grabbed a pencil and ran it along the teeth of the zipper. The graphite acted as a lubricant, and in seconds, the zipper glided open smoothly. This little hack saved me a lot of frustration and a few extra minutes.

The Joy of Simple Solutions: Why Life Hacks Matter

Life hacks are more than just quick fixes; they are creative ways to look at problems from a different angle. A simple trick can turn a stressful situation into a moment of triumph. Whether you're organizing your workspace or solving a tech issue, life hacks give you the tools to be more efficient, productive, and creative.

Key Hacks for Everyday Situations

Hack 1: The Coffee Spill Savior

We've all had that moment when a cup of coffee tips over, leaving a stain on the carpet or table. To quickly clean it up, sprinkle some baking soda over the spill and let it sit for a few minutes. Then, gently vacuum the area. The baking soda absorbs the liquid and odor, and your space is back to normal in no time.

Step-by-Step:

1. Immediately blot the spill with a paper towel or cloth to soak up as much liquid as possible.
2. Sprinkle baking soda generously over the spill.
3. Let it sit for about 10 minutes to absorb moisture.
4. Vacuum the area, and your surface will be spotless.

Hack 2: Organizing Cables and Chargers

Cables are notorious for becoming tangled and cluttered. A simple hack to organize them is using empty toilet paper rolls. Label each roll for different cables (e.g., phone charger, laptop cable) and store them inside a drawer. You'll be able to quickly find what you need without dealing with knots and tangles.

Step-by-Step:

1. Take an empty toilet paper roll and label it for each cable.
2. Coil each cable neatly and slide it inside the corresponding roll.
3. Store the rolls in a drawer or on a shelf for easy access.

More than Just Hacks: Creative Thinking for Problem-Solving

Every life hack is a tiny example of how thinking creatively can transform your environment and mindset. It's about seeing everyday objects for their hidden potential and making your life just a little bit easier.

Practical Scenario: The Leaky Water Bottle

Imagine you're on a long journey and your water bottle starts to leak. Instead of panicking, try placing a small piece of plastic wrap over the opening before screwing the cap back on. This will create a seal and prevent further leaks.

Step-by-Step:

1. Open the bottle and cut a small piece of plastic wrap.
2. Place the plastic wrap tightly over the opening.
3. Screw the cap back on securely.
4. This creates a temporary seal, stopping the leak.

Unlocking the Potential: Life Hacks at Work and Home

Life hacks are not limited to personal convenience. They can be applied at work, at home, and even while traveling. They help you streamline tasks, reduce clutter, and improve productivity.

Anecdote: The Drawer Disaster

One afternoon, I opened my office drawer to retrieve a pen, only to be faced with a pile of random objects—paperclips, receipts, sticky notes—everything jumbled together. Instead of spending an hour sorting through the chaos, I took a few minutes to use a few small boxes to organize everything. What was once a frustrating mess became an organized and easy-to-navigate space.

Conclusion: Embrace the Hack Life

Life hacks are all about transforming ordinary moments into opportunities for improvement. The joy of solving problems with simple solutions is not just about convenience; it's about cultivating a mindset that embraces creativity and efficiency. Whether it's organizing, cleaning, or managing everyday annoyances, these hacks are your ticket to a smoother, more enjoyable life.

Chapter Two

Kitchen Magic
Hacks for Cooking and Storage Mastery

Cooking and storing food doesn't have to be a chore. Discover a world of possibilities with these ingenious hacks to simplify your kitchen routine, save time, and make the most out of your ingredients and storage space.

Section 1: Freshness Hacks

Keeping ingredients fresh for longer can be a game-changer in the kitchen. These hacks help extend the life of your produce, saving you time and money.

Hack 1: Keep Herbs Fresh Longer

Fresh herbs are a staple in many kitchens, but they tend to wilt and spoil quickly. To preserve their flavor and vibrancy, wrap your herbs in a damp paper towel and store them in a reseal able bag in the fridge. This simple trick helps herbs stay fresh for weeks.

Anecdote: I used to waste so many fresh herbs because they would wilt within days of buying them. Then, I tried the damp paper towel trick, and it worked wonders. I could now enjoy fresh cilantro and parsley all week long, which made my cooking more flavorful.

Step-by-Step:

1. Take your fresh herbs and rinse them thoroughly if needed.
2. Lay them flat on a damp paper towel.
3. Roll the towel up loosely with the herbs inside.
4. Place the wrapped herbs in a resealable plastic bag and store them in the fridge.
5. Check every few days and re-moisten the paper towel if necessary.

Hack 2: Extend Fruit Shelf Life

Fruit, especially apples and bananas, can ripen too quickly, leading to waste. Try these simple tricks to slow down the ripening process and extend shelf life.

Step-by-Step:

1. Place apples and potatoes together in the fridge or pantry. The potatoes release gases that slow down the apples' ripening.
2. Store bananas in separate clusters rather than as a bunch. This helps slow their ripening by reducing the ethylene gas produced.

Section 2: Meal Prep Made Easy

Meal prepping can save time during the week, making dinner or snacks quick and easy. Here are a few hacks to streamline the process.

Hack 1: Portion Sauces with Ice Trays

Leftover sauces or soups can be frozen in an ice tray for convenient, ready-to-use cubes. This allows you to easily thaw just the amount you need for future meals.

Anecdote: I often had leftover marinara sauce after spaghetti nights, but I didn't want to waste it. Freezing it in ice trays allowed me to use just a cube or two whenever I needed a quick pasta topping, without having to cook a whole new batch.

Step-by-Step:

1. Pour leftover sauces or soups into an ice cube tray, filling each section.
2. Freeze the tray for several hours or overnight.
3. Once frozen, transfer the cubes into a freezer bag for easy storage.
4. Label the bag with the type of sauce for easy identification.

Hack 2: Pre-Chop Veggies

Chopping vegetables in advance can save time during meal preparation. Prep your onions, peppers, and carrots, and store them in airtight containers in the fridge for quick access.

Step-by-Step:

1. Wash and peel your vegetables.
2. Slice or chop them into your desired sizes.
3. Place them in airtight containers or reseal able bags.
4. Store the pre-chopped veggies in the fridge, where they will stay fresh for several days.

Section 3: Creative Storage Solutions

Get creative with your kitchen storage to maximize space and keep things organized.

Hack 1: Repurpose Egg Cartons

Egg cartons are perfect for organizing small items like condiments, spices, or fragile fruits in the fridge. They keep everything neat and prevent items from rolling around.

Step-by-Step:

1. Clean an empty egg carton thoroughly.
2. Use it to organize small jars of condiments or store delicate fruits like berries.
3. Label each compartment for quick access.

Hack 2: Label Everything

Labeling is essential for keeping track of the contents of your jars and containers. Use chalkboard labels or stickers that can easily be removed or rewritten to mark the contents.

Step-by-Step:

1. Purchase chalkboard labels or reusable stickers.

2. Write the contents of each jar or container with a chalk marker or permanent pen.
3. Stick the labels to the jars or containers.
4. When you finish the contents, simply erase or replace the label.

Section 4: Cleanup Tips

Cleaning doesn't have to be time-consuming. Here are a couple of quick hacks to make the process easier.

Hack 1: Quick Microwave Cleaner

Microwaves can get dirty quickly with splatters and spills. To make cleaning easier, place a bowl of water with lemon slices inside and heat it for five minutes. The steam will loosen grime, making it much easier to wipe down.

Anecdote: I used to dread cleaning my microwave because of all the sticky spots. But after discovering this trick, I now have a clean microwave in under 10 minutes.

Step-by-Step:

1. Fill a microwave-safe bowl with water.
2. Add several slices of lemon to the bowl.
3. Place the bowl in the microwave and heat on high for 5 minutes.
4. Once the microwave beeps, carefully remove the bowl and wipe down the interior with a clean cloth.

Hack 2: Grease-Proof Your Stove

To avoid scrubbing grease off your stove, lay aluminum foil beneath the burners. This way, when grease splatters, you can simply replace the foil instead of cleaning the entire stove.

Step-by-Step:

1. Cut a piece of aluminum foil to fit under your stove burners.
2. Place it under the burners, covering the surface.
3. When it gets dirty, simply remove the foil and replace it with a new sheet.

Conclusion: Kitchen Hacks for Everyday Ease

Mastering kitchen hacks isn't just about saving time—it's about making your cooking and storage experience more enjoyable. With these clever tricks, you can keep your ingredients fresh longer, simplify meal prep, and reduce cleaning time, all while maintaining a tidy and efficient kitchen. The magic is in the details, and with a little creativity, you can transform your kitchen into a well-oiled machine.

Chapter Three

Home Sweet Hacks

Solutions for a Tidier, Smarter Home

Your home should be your sanctuary, not a source of stress. With these clever hacks, you'll be able to organize and tidy your living space in ways that save you time, energy, and frustration. From hidden storage to decluttering techniques, let's explore simple solutions to help you transform your home into a more functional, stress-free space.

Section 1: Hidden Storage

Maximize the use of your space by hiding storage in plain sight. These hidden storage ideas will make your home look tidier while keeping your things organized and easily accessible.

Hack 1: Furniture with Dual Purpose

Ottomans and other furniture with hidden compartments are great for storing blankets, toys, or even seasonal clothing. These pieces serve as both functional furniture and discreet storage solutions.

Anecdote: I was tired of tripping over stray blankets and toys in my living room. After finding a stylish ottoman with hidden storage, I was able to stow everything out of sight, and the room immediately looked more organized and cozy.

Step-by-Step:

1. Choose a sturdy ottoman or coffee table with a lift-up or hidden compartment.
2. Use the compartment to store extra blankets, pillows, or children's toys.
3. For added convenience, line the compartment with fabric bins to further organize items inside.

Hack 2: Under-the-Bed Storage

The space under your bed is often unused, but it can be an excellent storage area for seasonal clothes, shoes, or extra bedding.

Anecdote: I always found it difficult to store bulky winter clothes when the weather changed. Once I started using flat storage bins under my bed, I could easily access my off-season clothes without taking up valuable closet space.

Step-by-Step:

1. Measure the height and length of the space under your bed to ensure the bins will fit.
2. Purchase low-profile storage bins that slide easily under your bed.
3. Store seasonal clothes, shoes, or extra linens in the bins.
4. Label the bins for easy identification.

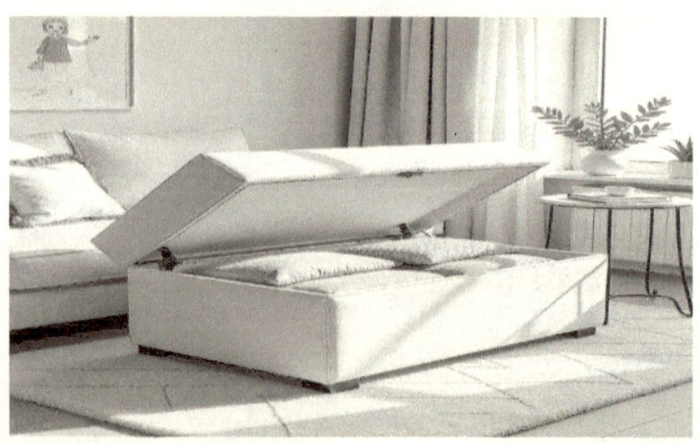

Section 2: Decluttering Tips

A cluttered space can feel overwhelming, but these quick and easy decluttering hacks will help you maintain a tidy home with minimal effort.

Hack 1: Tidy Drawers

Instead of folding clothes traditionally, rolling them allows you to see everything in your drawer at a glance and make more efficient use of space.

Anecdote: I used to struggle with drawers that were overstuffed, and it was a hassle to find anything. Rolling my clothes changed everything—now, I can fit more, and it's much easier to see what I have at a glance.

Step-by-Step:

1. Lay your clothes flat on a clean surface.
2. Starting from one end, roll the clothing tightly into a compact cylinder.
3. Place the rolled items in drawers vertically, rather than stacking them.
4. Arrange by type or color for even easier access.

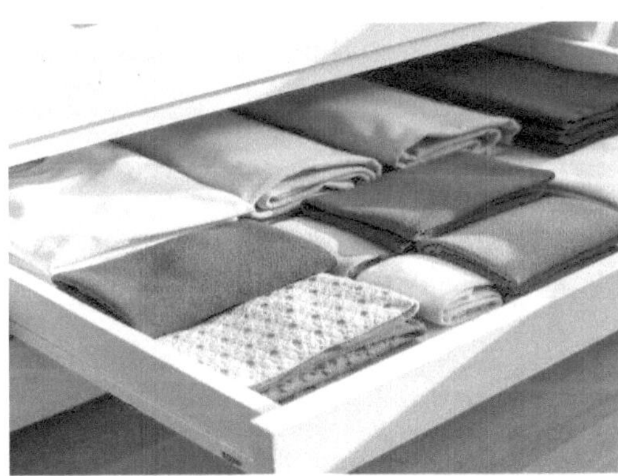

Hack 2: Five-Minute Cleanup Rule

The five-minute cleanup rule is simple: Spend just five minutes a day tidying up one area of your home. This quick habit prevents clutter from building up and makes cleaning less overwhelming.

Anecdote: I found it hard to keep my home consistently clean, so I adopted the five-minute rule. By focusing on one area for five minutes daily, I could maintain a clutter-free space without feeling like I was constantly cleaning.

Step-by-Step:

1. Set a timer for five minutes.
2. Choose one area of your home—whether it's your kitchen countertop, a bathroom shelf, or your entryway.
3. Quickly pick up clutter, put items back where they belong, and wipe down surfaces.
4. Repeat daily to keep things under control.

Section 3: DIY Organization Hacks

Organizing doesn't always require buying expensive products. These DIY hacks use everyday items to create effective, low-cost solutions.

Hack 1: Binder Clips for Cable Organization

Binder clips are inexpensive and easy-to-use tools for managing messy cables. Attach them to the edge of your desk or table, and loop your cables through the metal arms to keep them tangle-free.

Anecdote: I used to dread dealing with cables—my desk was always covered in a tangle of cords. Once I started using binder clips to organize them, my workspace became much cleaner and more functional.

Step-by-Step:

1. Gather a few large binder clips.
2. Attach the clips to the edge of your desk, shelf, or work surface.
3. Slip the cords through the metal arms of the binder clips to keep them neatly organized.
4. Label each clip with the corresponding device name for easy identification.

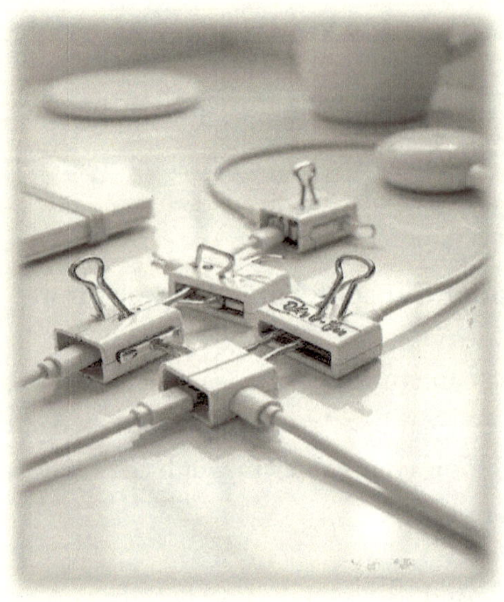

Hack 2: Repurpose an Old Shoe Rack for Cleaning Supplies

An old shoe rack can be a perfect organizer for your cleaning products. Repurpose it by placing bottles of cleaners, rags, and sponges in each section for easy access.

Anecdote: I was always fumbling through my kitchen cabinet trying to find my cleaning supplies. By using an old shoe rack, I could keep everything organized and within reach, making cleaning less of a hassle.

Step-by-Step:

1. Clean and prepare your old shoe rack for use.

2. Place your cleaning supplies in the slots—spray bottles, rags, sponges, and gloves.
3. If necessary, add labels to each section for quick identification.
4. Store the rack in a closet or utility room for easy access.

Conclusion: Home Hacks for a Calmer, More Organized Space

By implementing these simple yet effective hacks, you can turn your home into a clutter-free, organized haven. Whether you're maximizing hidden storage spaces, decluttering with easy techniques, or repurposing everyday items, these hacks will help you create a smarter, tidier home. And best of all, these ideas can save you time, reduce stress, and make your space more functional for everyday life.

Chapter Four

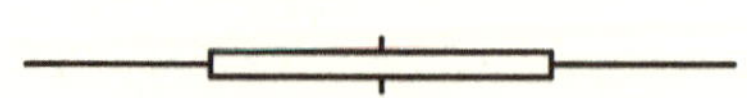

Tech-Savvy Tricks
Fixes and Boosts for Your Digital Life

In today's fast-paced digital world, it's easy to feel overwhelmed by technical glitches or slow devices. But with the right hacks, you can become the master of your gadgets. This chapter will guide you through device maintenance, simple DIY solutions, and clever tricks to optimize your digital life. Whether you want to speed up your laptop, tidy up your cables, or clean your keyboard, you'll find simple solutions that make a big impact.

Section 1: Device Maintenance

Keeping your digital devices in top shape doesn't have to be complicated. These simple maintenance hacks will help you extend the life of your devices and keep them running smoothly.

Hack 1: Keyboard Cleaning

Over time, keyboards collect dust, crumbs, and other debris, making typing a hassle. Regular cleaning can improve both appearance and performance.

Anecdote: I used to struggle with keys sticking because of all the crumbs and dust in my keyboard. After adopting this simple cleaning routine, my keyboard looks and feels like new!

Step-by-Step:

1. Turn off your device and unplug the keyboard if it's external.
2. Use a soft toothbrush to gently brush the keys and the crevices between them, removing dirt and debris.
3. For deeper cleaning, use a mini vacuum or compressed air to blow out any stubborn dirt particles.
4. Wipe the surface with a microfiber cloth to remove any remaining dust.

Hack 2: Speed Up Your Laptop

A slow laptop can be incredibly frustrating, but simple steps can boost its speed without needing any technical expertise.

Anecdote: I noticed my laptop becoming slower over time due to too many apps and files cluttering my desktop. By cleaning it up and removing unnecessary programs, my laptop became much faster and more responsive.

Step-by-Step:

1. Delete or move files you no longer need off your desktop to reduce clutter.
2. Uninstall any software or apps that you no longer use by going to your device's settings or control panel.
3. Run a disk cleanup to remove temporary files and free up space.
4. Consider upgrading your RAM or using an external hard drive for additional storage to boost performance.

Section 2: DIY Solutions

Sometimes, the best solutions come from repurposing everyday items. These clever DIY tricks help you stay organized and reduce tech-related stress.

Hack 1: Cable Organizers

Cables can easily become tangled, making it hard to find the right one when you need it. Repurposing toilet paper rolls is an easy and eco-friendly way to organize your cords.

Anecdote: I used to spend far too much time untangling my cables, but once I started using toilet paper rolls, I was able to keep all my cords organized and accessible.

Step-by-Step:

1. Collect a few empty toilet paper rolls.
2. Label each roll with the name of the device or cable (e.g., "Phone charger," "Laptop charger").
3. Slide the cords into the rolls to keep them from tangling.
4. Store them in a drawer or box for easy access.

Hack 2: Charging Station

Creating a dedicated charging station can help you keep your devices charged and organized. Using a multi-outlet power strip mounted to the side of your desk can streamline the process.

Anecdote: I was always searching for outlets to charge my phone, tablet, and laptop. Mounting a power strip on my desk made charging so much easier and kept my workspace clutter-free.

Step-by-Step:

1. Choose a power strip with multiple outlets that suits your charging needs.
2. Use adhesive hooks or a mounting bracket to attach the power strip to the side of your desk.
3. Plug in your chargers for easy access.

4. Use cable ties or clips to organize your cables and prevent them from tangling.

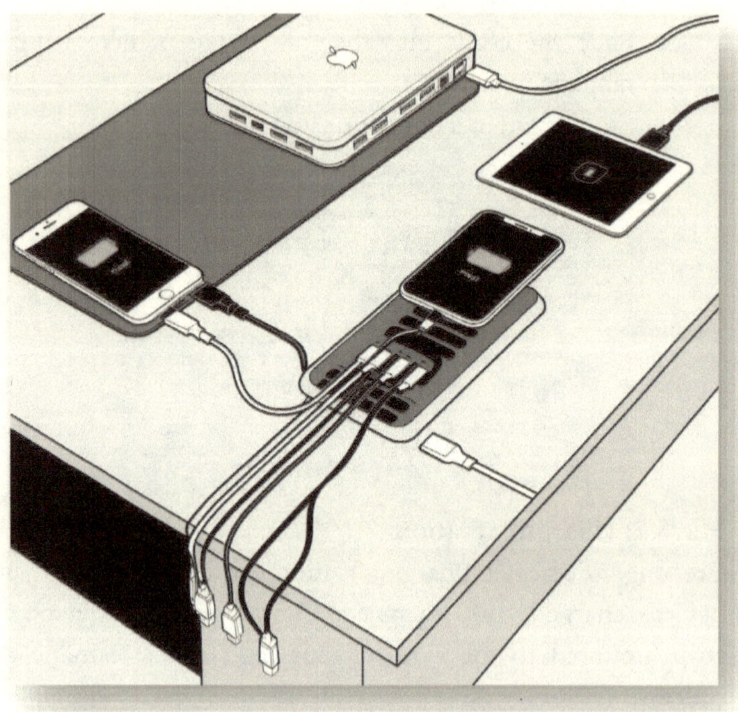

Conclusion: Tech Tricks for a Smoother Digital Life

By incorporating these easy-to-follow maintenance and DIY hacks, you'll be able to optimize your devices, stay organized, and improve the efficiency of your digital life. With a few simple changes, you can extend the life of your gadgets, make everyday tasks more convenient, and keep your workspace free from clutter.

Chapter Five

Wardrobe Wizardry
Clever Clothing and Laundry Solutions

Your wardrobe doesn't just store your clothes; it holds your confidence and personality. From dealing with stubborn stains to creating an organized closet system, this chapter offers simple yet effective hacks to keep your clothing fresh, neat, and easily accessible. Whether you need to remove a tough stain or find space for your accessories, these tricks will save time and energy.

Section 1: Laundry Tips

Laundry doesn't have to be a time-consuming chore when you have the right hacks. These simple tips will make laundry day a breeze, helping you keep your clothes looking their best.

Hack 1: Stain Removers

Tackling stains doesn't have to require harsh chemicals. Natural alternatives like baking soda and vinegar work wonders on tough stains.

Anecdote: I once spilled red wine on my favorite shirt at a dinner party, and I thought it was ruined. But with a simple mix of baking soda and vinegar, the stain disappeared like magic!

Step-by-Step:

1. Mix a paste using baking soda and water (about 2 tablespoons of baking soda with enough water to make a paste).
2. Apply the paste directly to the stain and let it sit for about 15-20 minutes.
3. After the paste dries, scrape it off gently and wash the item as usual.
4. If the stain persists, mix equal parts white vinegar and water, apply it to the stain, and wash again.

Hack 2: DIY Fabric Freshener

Keep your clothes smelling fresh between washes with a DIY fabric freshener using essential oils.

Anecdote: I was tired of buying expensive fabric fresheners that didn't last long. So, I made my own spray using water and essential oils, and now my clothes always smell like a spa!

Step-by-Step:

1. Fill a small spray bottle with water (about 2 cups).
2. Add 10-15 drops of your favorite essential oil (lavender, eucalyptus, or lemon work great).
3. Shake the bottle gently to mix.
4. Lightly spritz the fabric freshener onto your clothes, avoiding saturation.

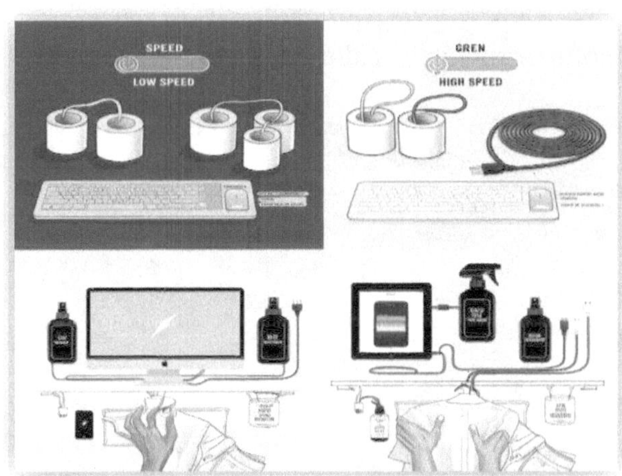

Section 2: Closet Organization

A cluttered closet can feel overwhelming, but with these simple hacks, you can easily organize and maximize your wardrobe space.

Hack 1: Accessory Storage

Small accessories like earrings, cufflinks, and rings can easily get lost in drawers. Using ice cube trays can keep everything neatly organized and visible.

Anecdote: I always lost my favorite earrings at the bottom of my jewelry box until I started using an ice cube tray to organize them. Now I can see exactly what I have!

Step-by-Step:

1. Find a clean, empty ice cube tray.
2. Place your small accessories (earrings, cufflinks, rings, etc.) into each compartment.
3. Keep the tray in your drawer, on your vanity, or in a closet for easy access.
4. For added organization, you can label the compartments or color-code your accessories.

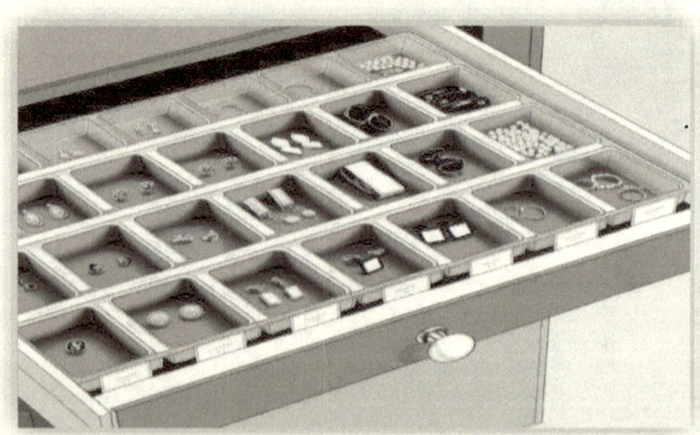

Hack 2: Hanger Tricks

Maximize your closet space by using shower curtain rings on hangers to store scarves, belts, or necklaces.

Anecdote: My scarves were always tangled, taking up too much space in my closet. Once I started using shower curtain rings, they hung neatly and were much easier to find!

Step-by-Step:

1. Take a sturdy hanger and attach several shower curtain rings to the bottom bar.
2. Hang your scarves, belts, or necklaces through the rings.
3. Organize by color or style for easy access.
4. Hang the modified hanger in your closet as you would any regular hanger.

Conclusion: Organize and Refresh Your Wardrobe

By incorporating these wardrobe and laundry hacks, you'll be able to maintain a clean, fresh, and organized closet without spending a lot of time or money. Whether you're tackling tough stains or finding new ways to organize your accessories, these tips will keep your wardrobe looking and feeling its best.

Here's an enhanced version of **Chapter 6: On-the-Go Genius: Hacks for Travel and Commuting**, with subheadings, anecdotes, step-by-step explanations, and detailed illustration prompts:

Chapter Six

On-the-Go Genius
Hacks for Travel and Commuting

Traveling should be exciting, not stressful. Whether you're jet-setting to a new destination or commuting daily, these life hacks will help you travel smart, save time, and ensure a hassle-free journey. From packing tips to creative solutions for keeping entertained on long commutes, these tricks will keep you prepared for every trip.

Section 1: Packing Tips

Packing smart can make a world of difference, saving you time and space while ensuring everything you need fits into your suitcase. Here are a couple of clever tricks to optimize your packing.

Hack 1: Roll, Don't Fold

One of the best ways to maximize suitcase space and minimize wrinkles is to roll your clothes instead of folding them.

Anecdote: I used to dread packing because I could never fit everything into my suitcase. Then, I learned to roll my clothes, and not only did I save space, but my clothes arrived with fewer creases!

Step-by-Step:

1. Lay out your clothing item flat (e.g., t-shirt, pants).

2. Starting from the bottom, tightly roll the item into a cylinder shape.
3. Stack the rolled items neatly in your suitcase. This method uses space efficiently and keeps clothes compact and wrinkle-free.

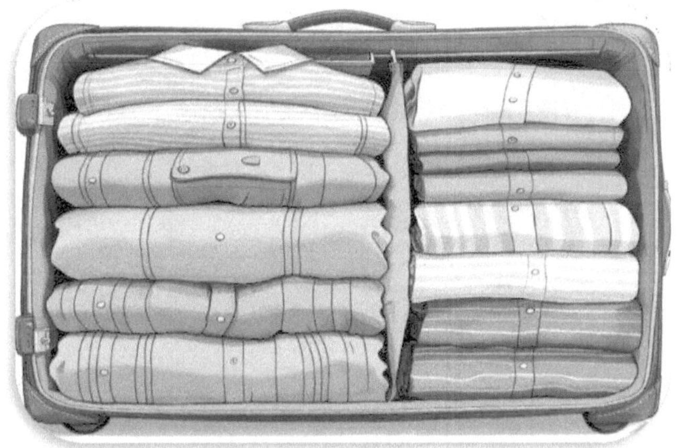

Hack 2: Organize with Zip Bags

Zip bags are a lifesaver for keeping toiletries, socks, and electronics organized. You can separate your items, making unpacking a breeze.

Anecdote: I used to toss everything into my suitcase and waste time searching for toiletries. Now, with zip bags, I can find everything in an instant, even at the bottom of my bag.

Step-by-Step:

1. Gather all your small items like toiletries, socks, and chargers.
2. Place each category in a separate zip bag (e.g., one for toiletries, one for socks, one for electronics).
3. Label the bags if needed for quick identification.
4. Put the bags in your suitcase, ensuring that the items you need first are on top.

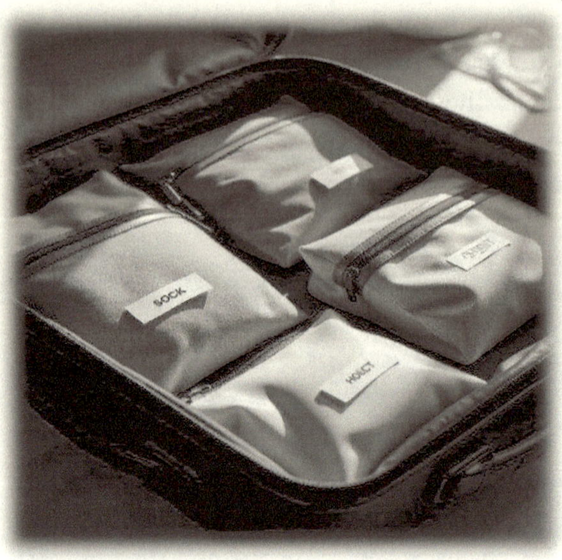

Section 2: Commuting Comfort

Long commutes can be tedious, but with a few hacks, you can make your journey much more enjoyable. Here's how you can add some comfort and convenience to your daily travels.

Hack 1: Portable Entertainment

Using a binder clip to hold your phone upright on a plane, train, or bus is an easy way to watch videos or catch up on your favorite shows without holding your device.

Anecdote: During a long train ride, I used to struggle with holding my phone in one hand while trying to enjoy a movie. Then, I discovered this simple binder clip hack, and now I can watch hands-free!

Step-by-Step:

1. Take a large binder clip and open it up.

2. Attach the binder clip to the edge of a tray table or your seat in front of you.
3. Slide your phone into the clip, with the screen facing outward.
4. Adjust the angle to your liking and enjoy hands-free entertainment!

Hack 2: Emergency Kit

Carrying a small pouch with emergency essentials can save you from unpleasant surprises during your commute or travel. Items like band-aids, snacks, and a mini flashlight can be life-savers when you least expect it.

Anecdote: Once, I got a small cut on my hand while traveling, and I had no band-aid. Since then, I always carry an emergency kit with band-aids, snacks, and other essentials, and it's helped me countless times.

Step-by-Step:

1. Find a small pouch or makeup bag.
2. Pack essential items like band-aids, a mini flashlight, hand sanitizer, a snack, and any medications you might need.
3. Keep the pouch in your backpack or carry-on, ensuring it's easily accessible in case of an emergency.

Conclusion: Travel Smart, Travel Happy

With these simple yet effective hacks, you'll be well-equipped to handle all aspects of travel, from packing to commuting. Whether you're trying to optimize your suitcase space or make your commute more comfortable, these tips will help you travel with ease and confidence.

Chapter Seven

Eco-Friendly Fixes
Green Hacks for a Sustainable Life

In today's world, living sustainably isn't just an option—it's a necessity. Whether you're looking to reduce waste, conserve energy, or repurpose everyday items, these eco-friendly fixes will help you live greener and waste less. Embrace the power of small changes to make a big impact on the environment

Section 1: Waste Reduction Hacks

Living sustainably starts with reducing the waste we produce. These hacks focus on minimizing single-use items and making the most out of what we already have.

Hack 1: Reuse Jars for Storage

Instead of throwing away old glass jars, reuse them for storing pantry items, small accessories, or homemade cleaning products.

Anecdote: I used to discard jars, thinking they were just taking up space. Once I started reusing them for things like spices, nails, and screws, I found they made great organizers!

Step-by-Step:

1. Wash and remove labels from old glass jars.
2. Use the jars to store grains, pasta, or small office supplies.

3. Label the jars if needed for easy identification.

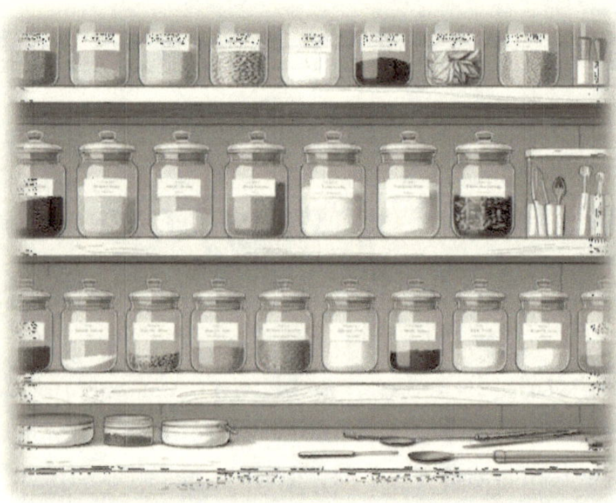

Hack 2: Cloth Napkins Instead of Paper

Switching from paper napkins to reusable cloth napkins can drastically cut down on your paper waste. Plus, they add a touch of elegance to every meal!

Anecdote: I used to go through rolls of paper towels every week. When I switched to cloth napkins, I not only reduced waste but also saved money in the long run.

Step-by-Step:

1. Purchase a set of cloth napkins or repurpose old fabric into napkin-sized pieces.
2. Use the napkins at every meal to replace paper napkins.
3. Wash and reuse the napkins instead of throwing them away.

Section 2: Energy-Saving Hacks

Saving energy is one of the easiest ways to reduce your environmental footprint. These energy-saving hacks will help you use less power and reduce your carbon footprint.

Hack 1: Unplug Devices When Not in Use

Many devices continue to consume power even when they are turned off. Unplugging devices when not in use can help save electricity and reduce energy costs.

Anecdote: I was surprised to learn that my charger was still using energy even when my phone wasn't plugged in. Now, I make it a habit to unplug devices after charging, and I've noticed a slight drop in my energy bills.

Step-by-Step:

1. Identify devices that are left plugged in but not in use (chargers, televisions, computers).

2. Unplug these devices when they're not in use, or use a power strip with an on/off switch to make it easier.
3. Consider using energy-efficient plugs or smart plugs that can be turned off remotely.

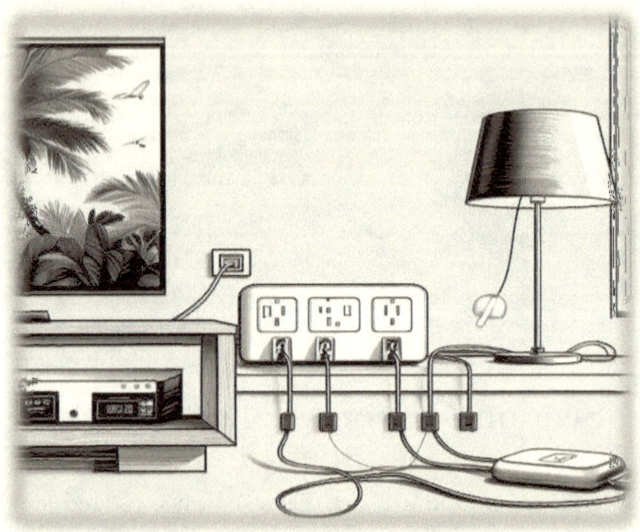

Hack 2: Use Energy-Efficient Bulbs

Switching to LED light bulbs is one of the easiest and most impactful changes you can make in your home. LED bulbs consume less energy and last longer than traditional incandescent bulbs.

Anecdote: After I replaced all my old bulbs with LEDs, I noticed a significant decrease in my electricity usage, and the bulbs lasted much longer than I expected.

Step-by-Step:

1. Replace all your incandescent light bulbs with energy-efficient LED bulbs.

2. Look for LED bulbs with the ENERGY STAR label to ensure maximum efficiency.
3. Consider dimmer switches to control lighting levels and save more energy.

Section 3: Eco-Friendly Cleaning Hacks

Green cleaning solutions are not only better for the environment but also safer for you and your family. Here are some cleaning hacks using natural, eco-friendly ingredients.

Hack 1: Homemade All-Purpose Cleaner

Skip the chemical-laden cleaners and make your own all-purpose cleaner using simple ingredients like vinegar, baking soda, and lemon.

Anecdote: I used to buy expensive cleaning products for every surface in my house. Once I started making my own cleaner, I saved money and reduced the number of harmful chemicals I used around my home.

Step-by-Step:

1. Mix 1 part vinegar with 1 part water in a spray bottle.
2. Add a few drops of essential oil (like lavender or lemon) for a pleasant scent.
3. Spray and wipe down surfaces like countertops, sinks, and mirrors.

Hack 2: Baking Soda for Stubborn Odors

Baking soda is a natural deodorizer that can be used to freshen up your home, from carpets to trash cans.

Anecdote: My refrigerator always seemed to have an odd smell. After I placed a small bowl of baking soda inside, the odor disappeared, and I didn't need to rely on store-bought deodorizers anymore.

Step-by-Step:

1. Place an open box of baking soda in your refrigerator, pantry, or other musty-smelling areas.
2. For carpets, sprinkle a small amount of baking soda, let it sit for 15 minutes, then vacuum it up.
3. Use baking soda as a natural deodorizer for shoes, trash cans, or even mattresses.

Section 4: Eco-Friendly Transportation

Transporting ourselves in a greener way can have a huge impact on our carbon footprint. These transportation hacks are simple and effective.

Hack 1: Ride a Bike for Short Trips
Instead of driving for short errands, consider riding a bike. It's a great way to reduce emissions and get some exercise.
Anecdote: I used to drive everywhere, even for short trips to the grocery store. Now, I bike whenever I can, and it's not only eco-friendly, but it also helps me stay active.
Step-by-Step:

1. Plan your route to nearby locations, like the grocery store or post office.

2. Make sure your bike is in good working condition—check the tires, brakes, and chain.
3. Keep a bike lock handy to secure your bike when you stop at your destination.

Conclusion: Small Changes, Big Impact

By incorporating these green hacks into your daily life, you can make a significant contribution to a more sustainable world. Remember, every little action counts—whether it's reducing waste, saving energy, or using eco-friendly products. The more we adopt these habits, the greater the positive effect we'll have on our planet.

Chapter Eight

Money-Saving Miracles Budget-Friendly DIY Solutions

Everyone wants to save money without compromising on quality or style. In this chapter, you'll discover clever, budget-friendly DIY solutions to stretch your dollars and still get the results you desire. From simple home repairs to creating personalized gifts, these hacks will help you live well on a budget.

Section 1: Home Repairs and Improvements

Why pay for expensive repairs when you can tackle them yourself? These DIY home fixes are easy, affordable, and surprisingly effective.

Hack 1: Fix a Leaky Faucet with Simple Tools

Instead of calling a plumber, fix a leaky faucet in just a few steps with basic tools. This will save you money on both the repair and the water bill!

Anecdote: I once had a faucet that dripped constantly. I was surprised how easy it was to fix—just a few turns of a wrench and the problem was solved. I saved a lot by avoiding the plumber's fee!

Step-by-Step:

1. Turn off the water supply to the faucet.
2. Use a wrench to remove the handle and access the cartridge.
3. Replace the worn-out washer or cartridge and reassemble the faucet.
4. Turn the water back on and check for leaks.

Hack 2: Patch Up Wall Holes with Toothpaste

Small holes in your walls don't need expensive spackling paste. You can use regular toothpaste to fill in small holes and cover them up temporarily.

Anecdote: When I moved into my apartment, I found a few small holes left by the previous tenants. I didn't want to spend much on repairs, so I used toothpaste. It worked great and kept the place looking neat!

Step-by-Step:

1. Squeeze a small amount of toothpaste onto a clean putty knife or your finger.
2. Press the toothpaste into the hole, smoothing it out until it's level with the wall.
3. Let it dry for a few hours, then lightly sand it for a smooth finish.
4. Touch up the paint if needed.

Section 2: Everyday Hacks for Saving Money

Everyday items can be repurposed or used more efficiently to save money. These clever ideas will help you make the most out of what you already have.

Hack 1: Make Your Own Cleaning Supplies

Skip buying expensive cleaning products by making your own with ingredients you probably already have in your pantry. It's cheap, easy, and effective!

Anecdote: When I first tried making my own cleaning supplies, I was amazed at how much I saved. Plus, I could customize the scent with essential oils, and I knew exactly what was in the products.

Step-by-Step:

1. For an all-purpose cleaner: Mix 1 cup of vinegar, 1 cup of water, and 10 drops of essential oil (like lemon or lavender) in a spray bottle.
2. For a glass cleaner: Combine 1 cup of water, 1 cup of rubbing alcohol, and 1 tablespoon of vinegar in a spray bottle.
3. For a bathroom cleaner: Use 1/2 cup of baking soda mixed with a little water to form a paste, then scrub.

Hack 2: Repurpose Old Clothes into Rags

Before you throw away worn-out clothes, consider repurposing them into cleaning rags or dust cloths. This will save you money on paper towels and make use of clothes that are too damaged to wear.

Anecdote: I used to toss out my old t-shirts, but now I cut them up and use them as rags for cleaning. It's a great way to reuse fabric and avoid buying paper towels.

Step-by-Step:

1. Take old, worn-out clothes like t-shirts, towels, or socks.
2. Cut them into small squares or strips, depending on your needs.
3. Store the rags in a basket or drawer and use them for cleaning, dusting, or as a makeshift mop.

Section 3: Frugal Food Solutions

Feeding yourself and your family on a budget doesn't mean sacrificing flavor. These food hacks will help you save money while still enjoying delicious meals.

Hack 1: Cook in Bulk and Freeze Leftovers

Cooking in bulk saves time and money. When you cook a large batch of food, you can freeze the leftovers for future meals, avoiding the need to order takeout or buy pre-packaged meals.

Anecdote: I started cooking large portions of pasta and stews and freezing the extras. It not only saved me time but also helped me avoid impulse takeout purchases. It's been a game-changer!

Step-by-Step:

1. Choose recipes that freeze well, like soups, stews, casseroles, or pasta dishes.
2. Cook in large batches and portion out individual servings.
3. Store the portions in airtight containers or freezer bags and label them with dates.
4. Reheat the frozen meals as needed.

Hack 2: Use Leftover Veggies for Homemade Soup

Instead of throwing away leftover veggies, use them to make a delicious homemade soup. This is a great way to save money while minimizing food waste.

Anecdote: I used to toss out leftover vegetables, but now I make a big pot of vegetable soup with whatever I have left. It's a great way to use up those scraps and create something nutritious.

Step-by-Step:

1. Gather leftover veggies like carrots, celery, onions, and potatoes.
2. Sauté the veggies in a pot with some olive oil, then add broth or water.
3. Let the soup simmer for 20-30 minutes, adding spices or herbs to taste.
4. Serve as a meal or store the extra in the fridge or freezer.

Section 4: Gift-Giving on a Budget

You don't have to spend a lot of money to give thoughtful and meaningful gifts. These DIY gift ideas will show you how to make memorable presents without breaking the bank.

Hack 1: Create Handmade Candles

Handmade candles make a thoughtful and inexpensive gift. Customize them with your choice of scents and colors for a personal touch.

Anecdote: I gave a homemade candle to a friend for her birthday, and she loved it! It was affordable, and I could customize the scent to something she enjoyed. It felt more personal than buying a store-bought candle.

Step-by-Step:

1. Melt soy wax in a double boiler.
2. Add a few drops of essential oil for fragrance and any color dye if desired.
3. Pour the melted wax into a small jar or container with a wick.
4. Let the candle set for several hours before gifting.

Hack 2: DIY Photo Frames from Recycled Materials

Instead of buying expensive frames, make your own with materials like cardboard, fabric, or even old magazine pages. These personalized frames will make your photos stand out.

Anecdote: I made a photo frame from an old cereal box and some scrap fabric. It turned out so well that I gave it as a gift, and my friend loved the creative touch!

Step-by-Step:

1. Cut cardboard into the desired shape and size for your frame.
2. Decorate the frame with fabric, magazine clippings, or paint.
3. Glue a photo onto the back of the frame and add a stand or wall hook for display.
4. Gift the frame with a favorite photo inside.

Conclusion: Small Savings Add Up

By incorporating these budget-friendly DIY solutions into your daily life, you'll not only save money but also develop valuable skills that will serve you in the long run. Remember, with a little creativity and effort, you can live well without spending big. Small changes lead to big savings!

Chapter Nine

Health and Wellness Wonders Simplifying Self-Care

Taking care of your health and wellness doesn't have to be complicated or time-consuming. This chapter is packed with simple and effective self-care hacks that will boost your physical, mental, and emotional well-being. Whether you're looking to improve your diet, get moving, or unwind after a long day, these hacks will help you feel your best every day

Section 1: Boosting Physical Health

Maintaining physical health doesn't require hours at the gym. These simple habits will keep your body strong and energized.

Hack 1: Energize with Morning Water and Lemon

Start your day with a glass of warm water and lemon. This refreshing drink helps jumpstart your metabolism, aids digestion, and boosts hydration.

Anecdote: I've been starting my mornings with lemon water for months now, and I notice a big difference in my energy levels. It's a small change, but it really sets the tone for a healthy day!

Step-by-Step:

1. Boil a small amount of water and let it cool slightly.
2. Squeeze the juice of half a lemon into the water.
3. Drink it on an empty stomach to hydrate your body and kickstart digestion.

Incorporating simple stretches into your daily routine can improve flexibility, reduce muscle tension, and increase overall energy.

Anecdote: I used to feel stiff after long hours at my desk. After adding a 10-minute stretching routine each morning, I noticed less discomfort and more energy throughout the day.

Step-by-Step:

1. Start with gentle neck stretches: tilt your head from side to side and forward and backward.
2. Stretch your arms overhead and side to side to loosen your upper body.
3. Focus on your legs: do standing hamstring stretches and calf stretches.
4. Finish with deep breaths to relax your body and mind.

Section 2: Nurturing Mental Wellness

Mental wellness is just as important as physical health. These simple hacks will help reduce stress, improve your mood, and enhance your overall mental clarity.

Hack 1: Practice Gratitude Every Day

Taking time each day to reflect on what you're grateful for can significantly boost your mental well-being. This simple practice helps shift your focus from negativity to positivity.

Anecdote: I started keeping a gratitude journal, and it changed my perspective. Writing down three things I'm thankful for every night helps me sleep better and feel more positive each day.

Step-by-Step:

1. Find a quiet moment each day to sit and reflect.
2. Write down at least three things you're grateful for, no matter how small.

3. Focus on how these things make you feel thankful and at peace.

Hack 2: Deep Breathing for Stress Relief

When stress starts to mount, taking a few minutes to breathe deeply can make a huge difference in how you feel. This simple relaxation technique calms the nervous system and helps reduce anxiety.

Anecdote: Whenever I feel overwhelmed at work, I take a short break to do deep breathing exercises. It only takes a few minutes but helps me refocus and feel more centered.

Step-by-Step:

1. Sit or lie down in a comfortable position.

2. Inhale deeply through your nose for 4 seconds.
3. Hold your breath for 4 seconds.
4. Exhale slowly through your mouth for 6 seconds.
5. Repeat for 3-5 minutes to calm your mind.

Section 3: Simple Self-Care for Relaxation

Self-care is essential for recharging, both mentally and physically. These easy self-care hacks will help you feel relaxed and rejuvenated.

Hack 1: DIY Spa Night with Natural Ingredients

Turn your bathroom into a spa by using natural ingredients to create your own face masks, scrubs, and body treatments. It's an affordable way to pamper yourself at home.

Anecdote: On busy weekends, I love treating myself to a DIY spa night. Using simple ingredients like honey, oatmeal, and coconut oil, I can make masks and scrubs that leave me feeling refreshed and glowing.

Step-by-Step:

1. Make a honey and oatmeal mask by mixing equal parts of honey and oats.
2. Apply the mask to your face and leave it on for 10-15 minutes.
3. For a body scrub, mix sugar or salt with coconut oil and exfoliate in the shower.

Hack 2: Sleep Sanctuary: Create a Relaxing Bedroom Environment

A good night's sleep is crucial for overall wellness. Make your bedroom a sanctuary by eliminating distractions and creating a calm, restful atmosphere.

Anecdote: I struggled with insomnia until I rearranged my bedroom to be more relaxing. With dim lighting, soft sheets, and no electronics, I now fall asleep faster and wake up feeling more rested.

Step-by-Step:

1. Keep your bedroom dark by using blackout curtains or a sleep mask.
2. Set a calming bedtime routine, such as reading or listening to soft music.
3. Remove electronics from the room, or at least an hour before bed.

Section 4: Nourishing Your Body with Food

Healthy eating is an essential part of wellness. These simple food-related hacks will nourish your body and keep you feeling energized throughout the day.

Hack 1: Make Smoothies for Quick, Nutrient-Packed Meals

Smoothies are an easy way to pack in a variety of fruits, vegetables, and protein in one meal. You can prepare them in minutes and enjoy a balanced meal on the go.

Anecdote: I started making smoothies for breakfast, and they've helped me feel more energized and full throughout the morning. I love experimenting with different fruits and veggies each day!

Step-by-Step:

1. Add 1 cup of milk or juice (dairy or plant-based) to a blender.
2. Toss in 1-2 servings of fruits (bananas, berries, etc.) and leafy greens (spinach or kale).
3. Add protein (yogurt, protein powder, or nut butter) and blend until smooth.
4. Enjoy immediately or store for later.

Hack 2: Hydrate with Infused Water for Extra Flavor

Add natural flavors to your water with infused fruits, herbs, and spices. This will not only help you stay hydrated but also make drinking water more enjoyable.

Anecdote: I struggled to drink enough water until I started adding cucumber and mint. It makes it so much easier to drink, and it's refreshing on a hot day!

Step-by-Step:

1. Choose fruits like lemon, berries, or cucumber, and herbs like mint or basil.
2. Slice the fruits and herbs and add them to a jug of water.

3. Let it infuse in the fridge for a couple of hours, then enjoy a refreshing and flavorful drink.

Conclusion: Simple Hacks for a Happier, Healthier You

Incorporating small, simple changes into your daily routine can have a big impact on your health and well-being. These health and wellness hacks will help you feel rejuvenated, balanced, and ready to take on whatever comes your way. Start with one or two of these ideas today, and see how they can improve your overall quality of life!

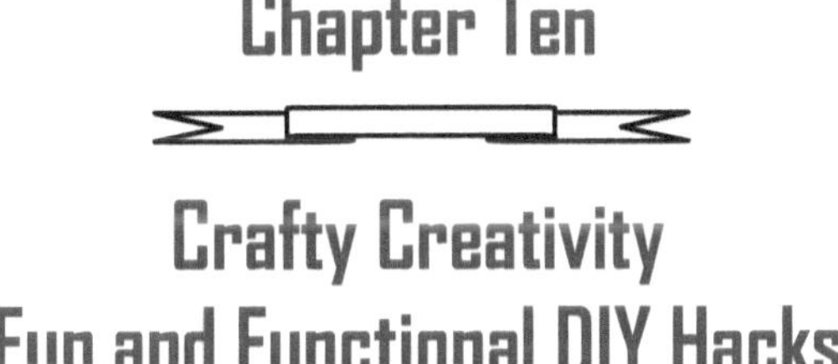

Crafty Creativity
Fun and Functional DIY Hacks

Unleash your inner creator with these fun and practical DIY hacks. This chapter shows you how to turn everyday items into extraordinary creations, giving you the tools to add a little creativity to your home, workspace, and life. Whether you're looking to craft unique decor, organize with style, or make functional items, these DIY hacks will inspire you to think outside the box.

Section 1: Upcycling and Repurposing

Repurposing items you already have is not only eco-friendly but also an opportunity to create something beautiful and functional from things that would otherwise go to waste.

Hack 1: Turn Old T-Shirts into Stylish Tote Bags

Instead of tossing old t-shirts, transform them into useful, eco-friendly tote bags. It's a simple way to create something practical and stylish from unwanted clothing.

Anecdote: I had a pile of old t-shirts that I no longer wore, so I decided to turn them into tote bags. It was so easy, and now I use them for shopping, carrying books, and even as gift bags!

Step-by-Step:

1. Lay the t-shirt flat, and cut off the sleeves and neckline.

2. Turn the shirt inside out and sew the bottom hem, or tie the fabric in knots to secure the bottom.

3. Turn it back to the right side, and your new tote bag is ready!

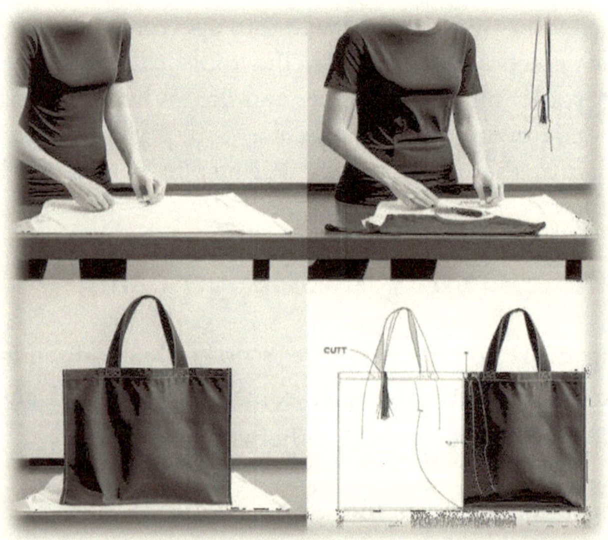

Hack 2: Make a Jewelry Holder from an Old Picture Frame

Give an old picture frame new life by turning it into a jewelry holder. This simple hack keeps your jewelry organized and adds a touch of vintage charm to your room.

Anecdote: I had a dusty old picture frame that was missing its glass, so I repurposed it as a jewelry holder. Now, I hang my necklaces and earrings on it, and it's both functional and decorative.

Step-by-Step:

1. Remove the backing from the picture frame and any glass or photo insert.

2. Attach hooks or nails across the frame for hanging necklaces, bracelets, or earrings.

3. Hang the frame on a wall or place it on a dresser for easy access to your jewelry.

Section 2: Fun Home Decor Ideas

Spruce up your home with budget-friendly and creative DIY decor projects. These hacks will help you add personal touches to your living space without breaking the bank.

Hack 1: Create a Mason Jar Candle Holder

Turn a mason jar into a cozy candle holder that adds warmth and charm to any room. This simple project is perfect for creating a rustic or vintage-inspired atmosphere.

Anecdote: I found a few old mason jars in my kitchen, so I decided to use them as candle holders. They not only look great but also create a soft, ambient light in my living room.

Step-by-Step:

1. Clean out the mason jar and remove any labels.
2. Place a small candle or tea light inside the jar.
3. Optionally, decorate the outside with twine, paint, or ribbon for extra flair.

Hack 2: Make Wall Art from Old Magazines

Transform your old magazines into a beautiful piece of wall art. This creative project gives new life to magazines and creates a custom, eclectic look for your walls.

Anecdote: I had a stack of magazines piling up, and instead of tossing them, I decided to create a collage. It's now one of my favorite pieces of art in the living room, and it cost me nothing!

Step-by-Step:

1. Cut out interesting images, words, or patterns from your old magazines.
2. Arrange the cutouts into a collage on a large piece of poster board or canvas.
3. Glue the images in place and frame your new artwork.

Section 3: Functional DIY Hacks

These functional DIY projects will help you organize, streamline, and improve the functionality of your home and workspace.

Hack 1: Repurpose an Old Ladder as a Shelf

Give an old ladder a new purpose by turning it into a rustic, multi-level shelf for books, plants, or decorative items. It's a unique way to add storage and style to any room.

Anecdote: I had an old wooden ladder in the garage that I was going to throw out. Instead, I gave it a fresh coat of paint and used it as a bookshelf. It's now a charming focal point in my living room!

Step-by-Step:

1. Clean and paint the ladder if needed to match your decor.
2. Lean the ladder against the wall or secure it for stability.
3. Use the steps as shelves to display books, plants, or other decorative objects.

Hack 2: Create a Cork Bulletin Board

Save your wine corks and use them to create a fun, functional bulletin board. This project is perfect for organizing notes, reminders, and photos.

Anecdote: After saving corks from wine bottles, I finally turned them into a bulletin board. Now, I can pin important papers and photos in a creative, eco-friendly way.

Step-by-Step:

1. Collect enough wine corks to cover a piece of cardboard or foam board.

2. Arrange the corks in a grid pattern on the board.

3. Glue the corks in place and let the glue dry before using it as a bulletin board.

Section 4: Clever Organization Hacks

Organization doesn't have to be boring. These hacks will help you keep your space tidy while also being creative and fun.

Hack 1: Use Shoe Boxes for Stylish Storage

Repurpose shoe boxes into stylish storage containers. With a little paint or wrapping paper, you can turn them into decorative boxes that store anything from office supplies to craft materials.

Anecdote: I was tired of my office supplies scattered around, so I turned a few old shoe boxes into storage containers. After decorating them with scrapbook paper, they look so much better than plain boxes!

Step-by-Step:

1. Collect shoe boxes and clean them out.
2. Decorate them with paint, fabric, or wrapping paper.
3. Use the boxes to store books, papers, or craft supplies.

Hack 2: Repurpose Jars for Office Storage

Old jars, like jam or mason jars, can be used to store pens, pencils, paper clips, and other office supplies. This hack is a great way to keep your desk tidy while adding a charming, handmade touch.

Anecdote: Instead of buying expensive desk organizers, I repurposed a few old jars into cute storage containers for my pens and supplies. It looks adorable and keeps my desk clutter-free!

Step-by-Step:

1. Clean out the jars and remove labels.
2. Fill the jars with office supplies like pens, paper clips, or scissors.
3. Arrange the jars neatly on your desk for easy access.

Conclusion: Embrace Your Inner Crafter

DIY projects are not only fun and rewarding, but they also help you transform everyday items into something new and useful. Whether you're upcycling, decorating, or organizing, these crafty creativity hacks will make your life a little more functional and a lot more fun. Start with one of these projects today and see how much your creativity can change the world around you!

Chapter Eleven

Kids and Pets
Easy Tricks for Your Little Ones

Life with children and pets can be both joyful and chaotic. From messy rooms to playtime disasters, it's easy to feel overwhelmed. But with a few clever tricks, you can simplify your daily routine and keep things running smoothly. This chapter offers creative solutions to help make life with your little ones and furry friends a little less stressful and a lot more fun.

Section 1: Kids' Care Hacks

Parenting comes with its own set of challenges, but these tips can help make things a little easier, from organizing toys to ensuring your child's clothes stay neat and tidy.

Hack 1: Turn Laundry Baskets into Toy Organizers

Toys can quickly take over your home, but using laundry baskets as toy organizers can help keep things in check.

Anecdote: When my child's toys began to fill every corner of our living room, I repurposed laundry baskets to keep them organized. Not only did it create a tidy space, but my little one could also easily find what they wanted to play with.

Step-by-Step:

1. Take a few laundry baskets (you can use different sizes depending on your child's toys).
2. Label each basket for different types of toys (e.g., stuffed animals, blocks, or art supplies).
3. Place the baskets in a designated play area, so toys are easy to grab and store.

Hack 2: Quick Cleanup with a DIY Toy Storage Bag

Instead of spending hours cleaning up toys, create a large, round storage bag that can double as a play mat. When playtime is over, simply pull the strings to gather everything into the bag.

Anecdote: Cleaning up after playtime was always a hassle until I made a large storage bag for my child's toys. Now, they can easily toss everything into the bag, and it's like a fun game!

Step-by-Step:

1. Cut a large piece of fabric (around 4 feet in diameter).
2. Sew a drawstring around the edge of the fabric.
3. Use it as both a play mat and a quick cleanup tool — pull the strings to gather the toys into the bag!

Section 2: Pet Care Hacks

Pets are a wonderful addition to any family, but they come with their own set of needs. These hacks will help make caring for your furry friends easier and more fun for both you and your pets.

Hack 1: Use a Shower Cap to Protect Furniture from Pet Hair

If your pet loves lounging on furniture, you know how much hair can accumulate. Instead of constantly vacuuming, try using a shower cap over your couch cushions to catch pet hair.

Anecdote: My dog sheds everywhere, especially on the couch. I started using a shower cap to cover the cushions when I wasn't around, and it saved me so much time on cleanup!

Step-by-Step:

1. Grab an inexpensive shower cap (preferably a large one that fits over your couch cushions).
2. Place the cap over the cushion when your pet is lounging on the couch.
3. Remove and clean the cap after the pet is done — this keeps your cushions hair-free.

Hack 2: DIY Pet Paw Cleaner

After walks in the dirt or mud, cleaning your pet's paws doesn't have to be a hassle. You can make a simple DIY paw cleaner using a jar and a few materials you probably already have at home.

Anecdote: After muddy walks, my dog's paws would get all over the house. I made a paw cleaning jar with water and a sponge, and it makes cleaning up after walks quick and easy.

Step-by-Step:

1. Fill a mason jar with warm water.
2. Add a soft sponge inside the jar (or a microfiber cloth).
3. After walks, dip your pet's paws in the jar, gently wipe them with the sponge, and dry with a towel.

Section 3: Harmonizing Kids and Pets

When kids and pets interact, there can be a lot of energy, noise, and potential chaos. These tricks can help you balance the two, keeping everyone happy and safe.

Hack 1: Teach Kids to Respect Pet Space with a "Pet Zone"

Teaching your children about respecting pet boundaries can help reduce stress for both the pet and the kids. Designate a specific area where your pet can retreat for quiet time.

Anecdote: Our dog loves playing with the kids but also needs some quiet time. We created a "Pet Zone" in a corner of the room where he can go to relax, and it's been a great way to teach the kids about boundaries.

Step-by-Step:

1. Create a small space in the home with a bed, blanket, or crate where your pet can relax.
2. Teach your child to recognize when the pet is in this space and needs quiet time.
3. Place a sign or soft boundary to help signal this space to kids.

Hack 2: Easy Pet Feeding Station with a DIY Dispenser

Organizing your pet's food and water doesn't have to be complicated. A DIY food dispenser can help manage portion control and keep feeding time clean.

Anecdote: We used to have food scattered everywhere, but with a DIY dispenser, it's now easier to measure out the right portions for our dog. It's helped reduce mess and keeps his feeding routine on track.

Step-by-Step:

1. Use a plastic bottle or cereal container and cut out a small opening for the food to pour out.
2. Attach a bowl beneath the container for easy access.
3. Fill the container with dry food, and use it to dispense portions directly into the bowl.

Section 4: Combining Fun and Learning for Both Kids and Pets

Life with both kids and pets doesn't have to be chaotic. With the right tricks and creative solutions, you can keep things calm, organized, and even educational.

Hack 1: Teaching Kids to Care for Pets with a Routine Chart

Kids can learn responsibility by following a routine chart for pet care. This simple tool helps them understand what tasks they can help with, like feeding, walking, or cleaning up after their pet.

Anecdote: I created a pet care chart for my child to follow, and it has made pet care a fun activity. My child loves ticking off the tasks each day, and it's great for teaching responsibility.

Step-by-Step:

1. Create a simple chart with tasks like feeding, walking, and brushing the pet.
2. Add pictures for each task so your child knows what to do.
3. Place the chart in a visible area where they can mark off completed tasks.

Conclusion: Making Life Easier with Little Ones and Pets

Caring for kids and pets doesn't have to be overwhelming. With these simple hacks, you can create a more organized, calm, and enjoyable environment for everyone. Whether it's managing toys, cleaning up after pets, or teaching kids responsibility, these tricks will help you streamline your daily routine and make the most of your time with your little ones and furry friends.

Chapter Twelve

Office Optimizers

Hacks for Productivity and Organization

A cluttered workspace can hinder productivity and make it difficult to stay focused. With these smart office hacks, you can optimize your workspace for maximum efficiency and stay organized throughout your workday. Whether you work from home or an office, these tricks will help streamline your tasks and make your environment a more productive place.

Section 1: Desk Organization Hacks

A tidy desk can boost productivity and creativity. Here are some simple ways to organize your desk to keep distractions at bay and improve workflow.

Hack 1: Desk Drawer Dividers for Easy Access

When you have a drawer full of office supplies, it can quickly become a jumbled mess. Using dividers can help you organize everything into categories, so you can easily find what you need.

Anecdote: I was always frustrated by the disorganization in my desk drawers until I added dividers. Now, everything from pens to paper clips has a dedicated space, making my day more efficient.

Step-by-Step:

1. Purchase drawer dividers (you can even use empty cardboard boxes if you're on a budget).
2. Organize supplies into categories: pens, sticky notes, paper clips, etc.
3. Label each section for even easier access.

Hack 2: Vertical File Organizers for Papers

Instead of stacking papers on your desk, use vertical file organizers to keep documents upright and easy to access.

Anecdote: My office used to be covered in stacks of papers, and it was overwhelming. By using vertical file organizers, I can quickly grab what I need without cluttering up my workspace.

Step-by-Step:

1. Get vertical file organizers or use magazine holders.
2. Categorize documents by type (e.g., bills, work assignments, reference materials).

3. Label each organizer so you know exactly where everything is.

Section 2: Time Management Hacks

Being efficient is all about managing your time wisely. Use these hacks to structure your day and eliminate procrastination.

Hack 1: The Pomodoro Technique for Focused Work

The Pomodoro Technique is a time management method that breaks work into 25-minute intervals (Pomodoros) followed by a 5-minute break. After completing four Pomodoros, take a longer break.

Anecdote: When I first started using the Pomodoro Technique, I was amazed by how much more I could accomplish in just 25-minute intervals. The key is to focus completely during those short bursts.

Step-by-Step:

1. Set a timer for 25 minutes and work on a task without distractions.
2. After 25 minutes, take a 5-minute break (stand up, stretch, grab a snack).
3. Repeat for four intervals, then take a 20-minute break.

Hack 2: Task Prioritization with the ABCDE Method

The ABCDE method is a simple yet powerful way to prioritize your tasks. This method helps you focus on what really matters and avoid wasting time on low-priority activities.

Anecdote: I used to waste time jumping between tasks without any sense of priority. When I started using the

ABCDE method, I could focus on what was important, and my productivity soared.

Step-by-Step:

1. Write down all the tasks you need to complete.
2. Assign a letter to each task:
    - **A** for tasks that are crucial (must be done today),
    - **B** for important tasks (should be done soon),
    - **C** for tasks that are nice to do (but not urgent),
    - **D** for tasks you can delegate,
    - **E** for tasks you can eliminate.
3. Start with the A tasks, then move on to the B tasks, and so on.

Section 3: Workspace Enhancements

Enhancing your workspace can help you feel more energized and motivated throughout the day. These hacks will help you create a comfortable, inspiring environment.

Hack 1: Cable Management for a Clean Desk

Cables can quickly clutter up your workspace, but with the right tools, you can keep them under control. Try using cable clips, zip ties, or a cable box to hide and organize cords.

Anecdote: I used to spend time untangling cables every day, but after I implemented a cable management system, my desk is much cleaner, and I feel more focused.

Step-by-Step:

1. Use cable clips to attach cords to the edge of your desk.
2. Bundle loose cables with zip ties or twist ties.
3. Store excess cables in a cable box to keep them out of sight.

Hack 2: Add Personal Touches for Motivation

Sometimes, a few personal touches can help motivate you and make your workspace feel more inviting. Try adding plants, photos, or motivational quotes to your desk.

Anecdote: I added a few plants and a motivational quote to my desk, and it completely changed how I feel when I sit down to work. The greenery is calming, and the quote keeps me focused.

Step-by-Step:

1. Place a small plant or succulent on your desk.
2. Add a photo or framed quote that inspires you.
3. Arrange your desk items so they inspire creativity and productivity.

Section 4: Digital Organization Hacks

With so many digital tools at your disposal, staying organized can be a challenge. These hacks will help you stay on top of your digital workspace.

Hack 1: Digital Declutter with Folders

Organizing your computer files into folders can drastically improve your workflow. This method allows you to quickly find what you need without endless scrolling through files.

Anecdote: I used to have a disorganized mess of files on my desktop, but after I created a folder system, I can now find anything in seconds.

Step-by-Step:

1. Create folders for major categories (e.g., Work, Personal, Projects).
2. Sort your files into these folders.
3. Name files clearly so you can easily search for them later.

Hack 2: Use Cloud Storage for Easy Access

Cloud storage services like Google Drive, Dropbox, or OneDrive make it easy to store and access files from anywhere. It also allows you to share files quickly with colleagues.

Anecdote: I used to struggle with transferring files between devices until I started using cloud storage. Now I can access my files anywhere, anytime.

Step-by-Step:

1. Choose a cloud storage service that fits your needs.
2. Upload important files to the cloud for easy access.
3. Organize your files within the cloud service with folders, so they're easy to find.

Conclusion: Transforming Your Office for Maximum Productivity

By implementing these office optimization hacks, you can create a more organized and efficient workspace. Whether it's organizing your desk, managing your time, or optimizing your digital tools, these simple tricks will help you stay on top of your tasks and feel more in control of your workday.

Chapter Thirteen

Outdoor Adventures
Camping and Gardening Solutions

Whether you're heading into the wild for a camping trip or sprucing up your garden, these outdoor hacks will make your adventures more enjoyable and efficient. From camping gear fixes to garden organization tips, these clever tricks ensure you're prepared for any outdoor challenge. Get ready to explore, relax, and create in the great outdoors.

Section 1: Camping Tips

Camping is an exciting way to reconnect with nature, but it can sometimes be tricky to manage all your gear. These hacks will help you make the most of your outdoor experience.

Hack 1: DIY Firestarter with Cotton Balls and Vaseline

Starting a fire when camping can be challenging, especially if the wood is damp. A simple DIY firestarter using cotton balls and petroleum jelly can help you create a quick and reliable flame.

Anecdote: On my last camping trip, the weather was damp, and lighting a fire seemed impossible. But thanks to my homemade fire starters, I had a warm campfire in no time.

Step-by-Step:

1. Take cotton balls and generously coat them with petroleum jelly.
2. Store the cotton balls in a Ziploc bag.
3. When you're ready to start your fire, fluff a cotton ball and place it under your kindling. Light it with a match or lighter.

Hack 2: Compact and Lightweight Cooking Kit

When cooking in the great outdoors, space and weight are crucial. Pack a compact, lightweight cooking kit that includes a small pot, collapsible utensils, and a multi-tool for all your food prep needs.

Anecdote: I used to struggle with overpacking for camping meals. Once I switched to a smaller cooking kit, I was able to enjoy a hot meal without the hassle of carrying bulky gear.

Step-by-Step:

1. Invest in collapsible utensils and a compact cooking pot.
2. Include a small cutting board, a multi-tool for chopping, and a lightweight stove.
3. Store everything in a travel pouch to keep it organized.

Section 2: Gardening Solutions

Gardening is a rewarding hobby, but it requires a bit of effort and organization. These hacks will help you maximize your space, keep your plants healthy, and reduce the workload.

Hack 1: Use Eggshells for Natural Fertilizer

Eggshells are a natural and eco-friendly fertilizer that can provide essential nutrients to your garden. Simply crush them and add them to your soil for healthier plants.

Anecdote: I started using eggshells in my garden last year, and I was amazed at how much my tomatoes thrived. The shells not only nourish the soil but also help keep pests at bay.

Step-by-Step:

1. Collect eggshells and rinse them clean.
2. Crush the eggshells into small pieces.
3. Mix the crushed shells into your garden soil or sprinkle them around the base of plants.

Hack 2: Create an Easy Vertical Garden with Pallets

If you're short on space but still want to grow a variety of plants, consider creating a vertical garden using wooden pallets. This is perfect for herbs, flowers, or even small vegetables.

Anecdote: I didn't have a lot of room for a garden, so I used an old pallet to create a vertical garden. It not only saved space but added a rustic charm to my backyard.

Step-by-Step:

1. Find an old wooden pallet and clean it up.
2. Attach plastic liners to the back of the pallet to hold soil in place.
3. Fill the pallet with soil and plant your choice of herbs, flowers, or small vegetables.
4. Place the pallet vertically against a wall or fence.

Section 3: Outdoor Organization Hacks

Whether you're camping or gardening, keeping your tools and gear organized is key to making your outdoor adventures more enjoyable. These hacks will help you stay on top of your equipment.

Hack 1: Use a Shoe Organizer for Outdoor Tools

An over-the-door shoe organizer isn't just for shoes! It can be used to store small tools, gardening gloves, and seeds, keeping everything easily accessible.

Anecdote: I used to lose track of my gardening tools, but with an over-the-door shoe organizer, I can now find my gloves, trowels, and seeds right when I need them.

Step-by-Step:

1. Hang a shoe organizer in your garage or garden shed.
2. Use each pocket to store tools like gardening gloves, small hand tools, or packets of seeds.
3. Label each pocket for easier identification.

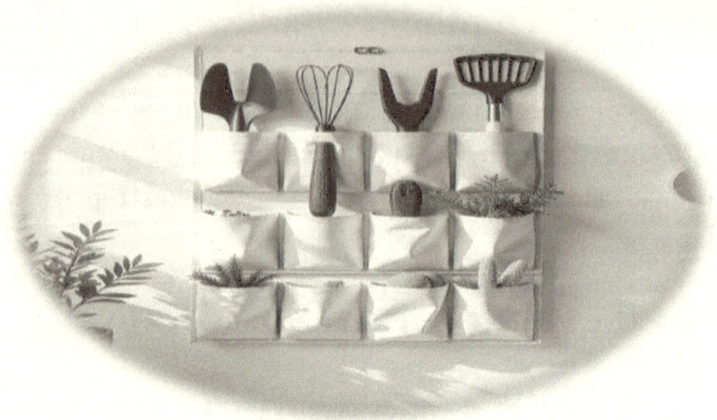

Hack 2: Repurpose a Bicycle Basket for Camping Gear

Repurposing an old bicycle basket is an eco-friendly way to carry and organize small camping gear, like lanterns, food, and utensils.

Anecdote: Instead of spending money on a new camping gear basket, I recycled an old bicycle basket. It holds everything I need and adds a charming touch to my camping setup.

Step-by-Step:

1. Find an old bicycle basket and clean it out.
2. Attach the basket to a sturdy part of your camping setup (like the side of your backpack or a shelf in your car).
3. Use it to store smaller camping items such as snacks, utensils, or batteries.

Chapter Thirteen

Conclusion: Embrace the Outdoors with These Clever Hacks

With these practical and creative outdoor hacks, you're ready to enjoy your camping and gardening adventures without the stress of disorganization or inefficiency. From firestarting tricks to gardening solutions and outdoor organization, these hacks will help you make the most of your time outdoors.

Chapter Fourteen

Quick Fixes
Instant Solutions for Everyday Problems

Life is full of little problems that can seem like big obstacles. But with a bit of ingenuity, you can fix almost anything in no time. Whether you're dealing with a broken zipper, a leaky faucet, or a wardrobe malfunction, these quick hacks will save the day. These emergency fixes will ensure you're always prepared for life's little mishaps.

Section 1: Household Emergency Hacks

When things break or go wrong at home, it's easy to feel overwhelmed. But with these quick fixes, you'll be able to handle household emergencies with ease.

Hack 1: Fix a Stuck Zipper with Soap

A stuck zipper can be incredibly frustrating, but there's a quick fix using something you probably already have in your home—soap. It's an easy way to get that zipper gliding smoothly again.

Anecdote: I once got caught in a rainstorm, and my jacket's zipper got stuck. I didn't want to spend time fumbling with it, so I quickly rubbed a bar of soap along the teeth, and it worked like a charm!

Step-by-Step:

1. Take a bar of soap (or a lip balm stick if you don't have soap handy).
2. Rub it along the zipper teeth, ensuring a light coating.
3. Gently move the zipper up and down until it slides smoothly.

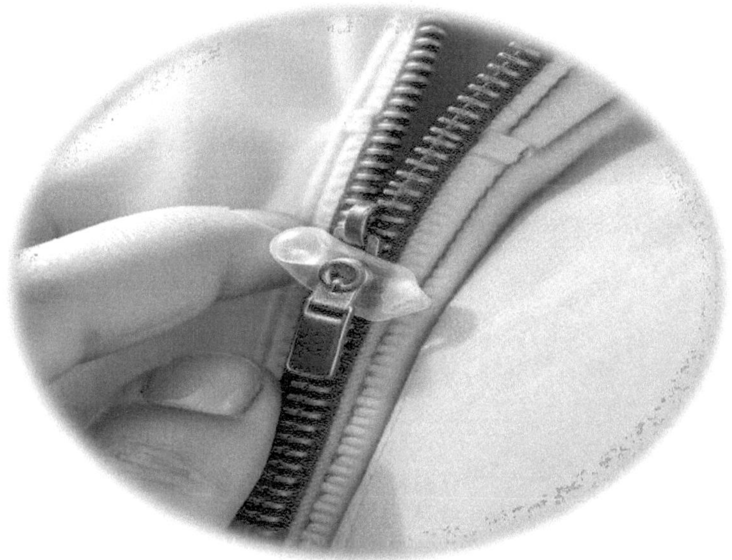

Hack 2: Unclog a Sink with Baking Soda and Vinegar

A clogged sink can quickly turn into a major inconvenience. Thankfully, you can clear it up quickly using baking soda and vinegar—a natural and eco-friendly solution.

Anecdote: After noticing my kitchen sink draining slowly, I remembered this simple trick. Within minutes, the clog was gone, and the sink was as good as new!

Step-by-Step:

1. Pour 1 cup of baking soda down the drain.
2. Follow with 1 cup of white vinegar.
3. Cover the drain with a cloth or plug and let the mixture sit for 15-20 minutes.
4. Flush with hot water to clear the clog.

Hack 3: Fix a Squeaky Door with Petroleum Jelly

Squeaky doors can be annoying, but they're easy to fix with a little petroleum jelly. This hack will help you silence that squeak instantly.

Anecdote: My front door used to squeak every time I opened it, especially late at night when I didn't want to wake anyone. A quick dab of petroleum jelly on the hinges solved the problem right away!

Step-by-Step:

1. Open the door and locate the hinges.
2. Apply a small amount of petroleum jelly to the hinge pins.
3. Open and close the door a few times to work the jelly into the hinges.

Section 2:

Wardrobe Fixes for Last-Minute Situations

From spills to wardrobe malfunctions, these quick fixes will help you look your best, even when you're in a pinch.

Hack 1: Remove Wrinkles with a Hairdryer

When you're in a rush and don't have an iron, a hairdryer can be your best friend. Use it to quickly smooth out wrinkles in your clothes.

Anecdote: I was running late for a meeting when I realized my shirt was wrinkled. I had no time to iron it, so I grabbed my hairdryer. It worked perfectly, and I was out the door in no time!

Step-by-Step:

1. Hang your wrinkled clothing on a hanger.
2. Hold the hairdryer about 6 inches from the fabric and turn it on the hot setting.
3. Move the hairdryer over the wrinkles, and they'll disappear almost instantly.

Hack 2: Remove a Stain with Baking Soda and Water

For those unavoidable spills, you can quickly remove a stain from your clothes using baking soda and water. It's a quick and simple solution for minor stains.

Anecdote: I spilled coffee on my white shirt during a morning meeting, but I used this quick hack to remove the stain before anyone noticed. It saved my day!

Step-by-Step:

1. Sprinkle a small amount of baking soda over the stain.
2. Add a few drops of water to create a paste.
3. Gently rub the paste into the fabric and let it sit for a few minutes.
4. Rinse the area with water or wipe it clean.

Hack 3: Stretch Tight Shoes with a Freezer Bag

If your shoes are too tight, you can easily stretch them out with a freezer bag filled with water. This simple method will give you a little extra room for comfort.

Anecdote: I bought a beautiful pair of shoes online, but they were a bit too tight. By using the freezer bag trick, I managed to make them fit perfectly without damaging the leather.

Step-by-Step:

1. Fill a freezer bag with water and seal it tightly.
2. Place the bag inside the shoe, ensuring it fills up the toe area.
3. Put the shoes in the freezer overnight. As the water freezes, it will expand, gently stretching the shoe.
4. Remove the bag in the morning and let the shoes thaw before wearing them.

Section 3: Quick Fixes for Digital Life

Technology can be frustrating when things go wrong, but with these emergency fixes, you'll be back on track in no time.

Hack 1: Charge Your Phone Faster with Airplane Mode

When you're in a hurry and need your phone to charge faster, switch it to airplane mode. This disables all non-essential services, allowing your battery to charge more quickly.

Anecdote: I was at an airport with only a few minutes to charge my phone. By turning on airplane mode, I was able to get enough charge to last the flight.

Step-by-Step:

1. Swipe down from the top of your phone screen to access quick settings.
2. Tap the airplane mode icon to enable it.
3. Plug in your phone, and it will charge faster than usual.

Hack 2: Fix Slow Internet with a Restart

If your internet is running slowly, sometimes all it takes is a simple restart of your router. This can resolve most connection issues instantly.

Anecdote: My internet connection was acting up during an important video call, but after restarting the router, everything was back to normal within minutes.

Step-by-Step:

1. Unplug your router from the power source.
2. Wait for 30 seconds, then plug it back in.
3. Wait for the lights to return to their normal state, and your internet should be faster.

Chapter Fourteen

Conclusion: Quick Fixes That Save the Day

With these quick fixes, you're now armed with solutions for everyday problems, from household mishaps to wardrobe malfunctions and tech issues. Whether you're dealing with a stuck zipper or a slow internet connection, these simple hacks will help you get back on track in no time. Life doesn't have to be complicated—sometimes, the best solutions are the simplest ones.

Chapter Fifteen

Hack Craft Toolkit Essentials You'll Need

Before you embark on your DIY and life-hacking journey, it's important to have the right tools and materials at your disposal. This chapter will guide you through the essentials every hacker should have in their toolkit. Whether you're fixing a leaky faucet, organizing your home, or crafting a new project, these items will make your life easier and your hacks more efficient.

Section 1: Basic Tools for Everyday Hacks

These versatile tools are the backbone of any home hack. They can be used for everything from quick fixes to DIY projects, ensuring you're always prepared for life's little challenges.

Hack 1: Multi-Tool

A multi-tool is a must-have for any DIY enthusiast. With options for cutting, screwing, and opening, it's the perfect tool for when you need a quick fix on the go.

Anecdote: I once found myself stuck in the middle of a camping trip when my flashlight's battery compartment wouldn't open. Thankfully, my multi-tool had the exact screwdriver I needed to open it and replace the batteries.

Step-by-Step:

1. Keep a multi-tool in your car, backpack, or tool drawer for quick fixes.
2. Use it for small tasks like tightening screws, cutting cords, or opening packages.
3. The compact design ensures it won't take up too much space.

Hack 2: Hot Glue Gun

A hot glue gun is indispensable for crafting, repairing, and even organizing. It bonds a variety of materials quickly and securely, making it a go-to for countless hacks.

Anecdote: I once used a hot glue gun to secure a decorative piece on my bookshelf that had come loose. The bond was so strong, it's still holding today, months later!

Step-by-Step:

1. Insert a glue stick into the gun and plug it in to heat up.
2. Apply the melted glue to your materials, quickly press them together before the glue sets.
3. Let the glue dry completely before moving the item.

Hack 3: Utility Knife

A utility knife is perfect for cutting through tougher materials, such as cardboard, plastic, or fabric. Its precision and versatility make it one of the most reliable tools in your kit.

Anecdote: When I needed to open a package quickly during a busy workday, my utility knife came to the rescue, making the process smooth and easy.

Step-by-Step:

1. Keep a utility knife on hand for cutting packaging, crafting projects, or even trimming fabric.
2. Make sure to retract the blade when not in use for safety.
3. Replace the blade when it starts to get dull for continued precision.

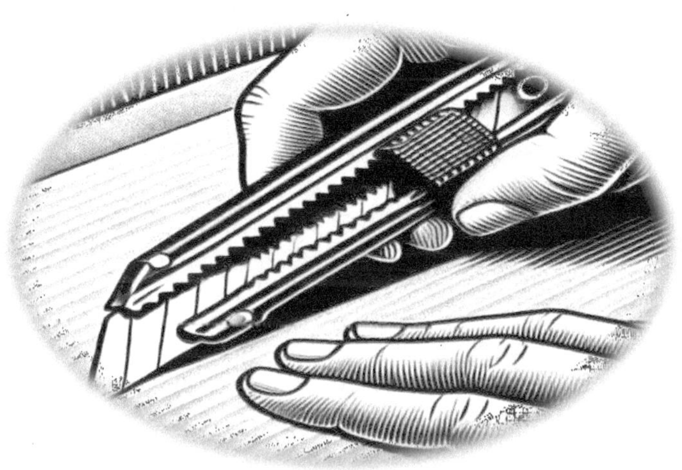

Section 2: Materials for DIY Projects

Once you have the right tools, it's time to stock up on materials. These essentials will help you complete a wide range of DIY projects, from home repairs to personal crafts.

Hack 1: Duct Tape

Duct tape is often called the "toolbox in a roll." It's incredibly versatile and can be used for anything from quick fixes to creating temporary solutions.

Anecdote: I once had a small tear in my favorite jacket, and duct tape saved the day! I applied it on the inside of the fabric, and it lasted through an entire camping trip.

Step-by-Step:

1. Keep a roll of duct tape in your car, toolbox, or home.
2. Use it to seal packages, repair cracks, or even temporarily hold things in place.
3. Its waterproof properties make it perfect for outdoor use as well.

Hack 2: Zip Ties

Zip ties are an incredibly useful way to organize cables, secure items, and even hold things together in emergencies. They're cheap, effective, and take up very little space.

Anecdote: I once had to secure a broken piece of luggage during a flight. Using zip ties, I was able to ensure it stayed intact until I could get home and fix it properly.

Step-by-Step:

1. Use zip ties to bundle cords together, keeping cables neat and tangle-free.
2. Securely fasten items that need temporary support, like a broken handle or a loose panel.
3. Cut the excess length of the zip tie once it's tight and in place.

Hack 3: Painter's Tape

Painter's tape is perfect for creating clean lines when painting, but it can also be used for other projects. It's gentle on surfaces, ensuring you don't damage anything during your hack.

Anecdote: I used painter's tape when I was re-organizing my office, ensuring the edges of my shelves and drawers remained clean while I was labeling them.

Step-by-Step:

1. Use painter's tape to create sharp lines or protect surfaces during a painting project.
2. Apply it to surfaces to prevent damage when scraping or drilling.
3. Remove the tape slowly to avoid peeling off any paint or finishes.

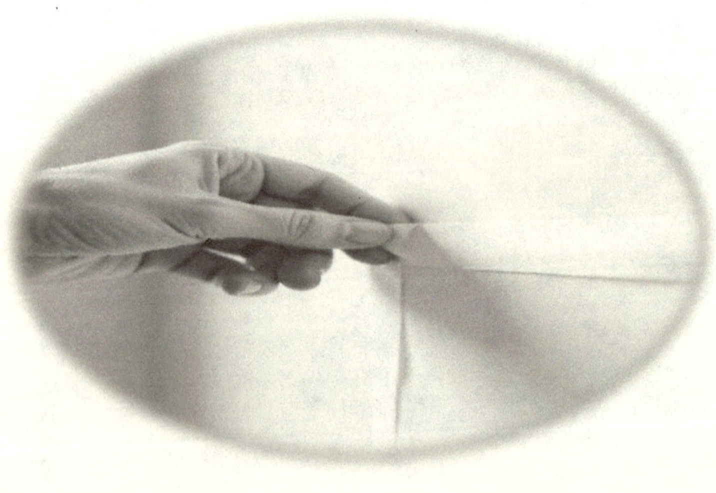

Section 3: Organizational Tools

A well-organized workspace is essential for efficient hacking. These items will help you keep your materials and tools in check, ensuring you can always find what you need.

Hack 1: Tool Box or Organizer

A sturdy toolbox or organizer is essential for keeping your tools and materials in one place. It will help you stay organized and make it easier to find the right tool when you need it.

Anecdote: My toolbox saved me so much time during a home renovation. I had everything neatly organized, so I didn't waste time searching for screws or a hammer.

Step-by-Step:

1. Use compartments to store small tools like screws, nails, and measuring tape.
2. Label each section so you can quickly find what you need.
3. Choose a portable toolbox to easily take your tools with you for on-the-go projects.

Hack 2: Clear Storage Bins

Clear storage bins are ideal for storing materials and tools. They allow you to see exactly what's inside, which helps save time when you're looking for something specific.

Anecdote: I use clear storage bins to store all my craft materials. It's so much easier to find what I need, and I can stack them neatly in a closet.

Step-by-Step:

1. Label each bin with its contents, such as "Craft Supplies" or "Electrical Tools."
2. Stack the bins for easy storage and access.
3. Use smaller bins for tiny items, like screws or nails.

Conclusion: Building Your HackCraft Toolkit

With the right tools and materials, you'll be ready to tackle any hack or DIY project that comes your way. From basic tools like multi-tools and glue guns to organizational items like storage bins, these essentials will ensure your hacking journey is efficient and fun. As you expand your toolkit, you'll be able to take on even more complex projects and create solutions for everyday problems with ease. Happy hacking!

Author's Note

As someone who has always been curious about finding smarter, simpler ways to tackle life's challenges, I've spent years observing, experimenting, and learning from the ingenious tricks people use to make their lives easier. This book is the result of that journey—a collection of practical, creative, and sometimes unconventional solutions designed to help you navigate the complexities of daily life.

The idea behind *HackCraft* is simple: life doesn't have to be as complicated as it seems. Often, the answers to our problems are hiding in plain sight, waiting for a bit of curiosity and creativity to uncover them. Whether it's streamlining your routines, solving common household dilemmas, or thinking outside the box to overcome obstacles, this book is here to inspire you to see challenges as opportunities for clever solutions.

These hacks are not just about convenience; they're about reclaiming time, energy, and mental clarity so you can focus on what truly matters. I hope this book sparks ideas, makes you smile, and perhaps even changes the way you approach the small (and big) problems in your life.

Happy hacking
Md Abdul Mannan

Acknowledgment

No journey is ever walked alone, and this book is no exception. *HackCraft* would not have been possible without the inspiration, support, and contributions of many wonderful individuals.

To my family, thank you for your unwavering encouragement and belief in my ideas, no matter how unconventional they might have seemed. Your patience, love, and understanding have been my greatest motivation.

To my friends and colleagues, who shared their own clever hacks and practical wisdom, your insights have enriched this book in countless ways. Your willingness to brainstorm, test ideas, and provide feedback has been invaluable.

To my readers, thank you for trusting me to bring solutions into your lives. It is your curiosity and desire to find better ways of living that inspire me to write.

Finally, my deepest gratitude goes to all the creative minds out there who see the world differently—problem solvers, tinkerers, and innovators. Your ingenuity fuels the very spirit of *HackCraft.*

This book is for all of you. Together, we can embrace life's challenges with curiosity, creativity, and a touch of cleverness.

Md Abdul Mannan

About the Author

Md Abdul Mannan is a writer, teacher, and perpetual seeker of creative solutions to life's everyday challenges. With a diverse background that spans education, literature, and an enduring curiosity for human behavior, he brings a unique perspective to problem-solving.

As an English teacher and storyteller, he has dedicated his life to empowering others through knowledge and creativity. His writing reflects his passion for uncovering ingenious ways to simplify life and make it more fulfilling. Through his books, he hopes to inspire readers to embrace curiosity, think outside the box, and find joy in solving even the most mundane problems.

When he's not writing or teaching, Md Abdul Mannan enjoys exploring new ideas, spending time with his family, and dreaming up fresh projects that merge practicality with creativity. *HackCraft* is a testament to his belief that with a little ingenuity, we can all lead more efficient and enjoyable lives.

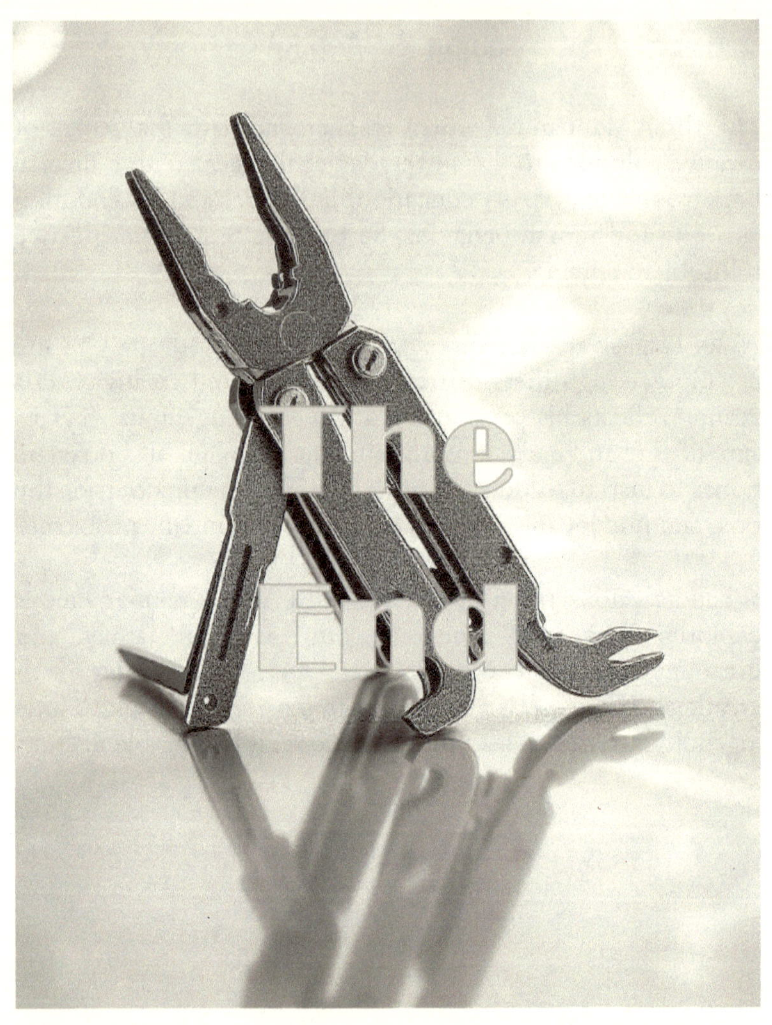
The
End

www.ingramcontent.com/pod-product-compliance
Lightning Source LLC
La Vergne TN
LVHW091102150826
845673LV00002B/691
* 9 7 9 8 2 2 7 2 5 6 5 2 2 *